Dramatic Diamonds

Written by Anne Marie Parker

CONTENTS

Dramatic Diamonds	2
What Is a Diamond?	4
Looking for Diamonds	6
Sparkling Diamonds	8
Famous Diamonds	10
Working With Diamonds	12
Growing Diamonds	16
Index	17

Dramatic Diamonds

For thousands of years people have been dazzled by the beauty of diamonds. But diamonds are also admired for their strength. They are the strongest mineral on Earth. That is why they are used in space, surgery and industry.

The Crown Jewels

Did you know?
a carat is a unit of weight for measuring diamonds equal to 200 milligrams

diamond-coated space craft

Fact Box:

Spoonmaker's Diamond
86 carats (17 grams)
Topkapi Palace Museum, Istanbul

One story says the Spoonmaker's diamond was found on the seashore by a fisherman. The fisherman traded the diamond to a jeweller for 3 spoons. Another story is that the diamond was found by a spoonmaker.

What Is a Diamond?

Diamonds are crystals. They are made up of the element carbon. Diamonds are formed deep within the earth's core when carbon is heated to a very high temperature and has a lot of pressure put on it.

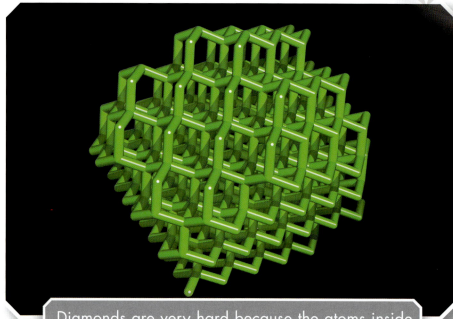

Diamonds are very hard because the atoms inside them are very strongly joined under pressure.

Glossary

carbon: a non-metal substance found in diamonds
crystal: a special mineral or stone
pressure: a continuous force put on an object by another

Fact Box

Hope Diamond
45.5 carats (9.1 grams)
Smithsonian Natural History Museum
Washington D.C.

The diamond is famous for the curse it is supposed to put on the person who possesses it. Found in India and said at one time to belong to Marie Antoinette. Many of the diamond's owners have died under strange circumstances.

Looking for Diamonds

Over many thousands of years, diamonds are pushed closer towards the surface of the earth. Then they can be mined or found in stream beds. Diamonds that are found in streams are called alluvial diamonds.

alluvial diamonds

Kimberlite Pipe

Kimberlite pipes are formed by molten lava forced upward from the earth's core. Over millions of years, erosion takes the tops off these kimberlite pipes. This exposes alluvial diamonds often found in swamps and rivers.

river

swamp

the earth's core

alluvial diamonds

looking for alluvial diamonds

Sparkling Diamonds

Diamond cutters cut and polish diamonds to make them sparkle and shine. A diamond cutter studies the diamond to find out the best places to cut it. Their cutting tools need to be very strong and sharp. That is why their tools are usually made from diamonds.

> **Fact Box**
> To produce the best sparkle, diamond cutters use the "brilliant cut", which has 58 sides, or facets.

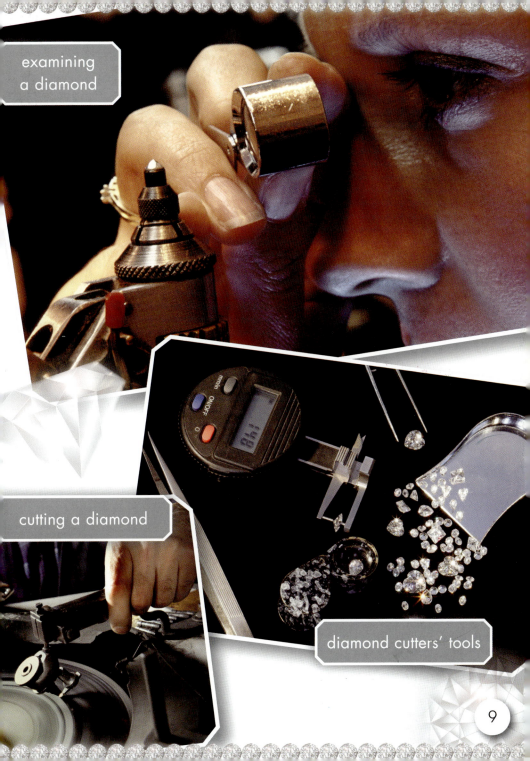

examining a diamond

cutting a diamond

diamond cutters' tools

Famous Diamonds

Throughout history, famous diamonds have been worn by important and wealthy people. Some of these diamonds are so expensive, they are kept in safe places and are well protected.

The largest diamond ever found was the Cullinan diamond which weighed 3,106 carats (600 grams).

A famous French emperor wore a sword set with the Regent diamond when he went in to battle to bring him good luck.

Fact Box
Regent Diamond
140.5 carats (28 grams)
Louvre Museum
Paris

Part of the French Crown Jewels, it was once worn by Napoleon and Marie Antoinette. It has been on display at the Louvre Museum since 1887.

Emperor Napoleon Bonaparte

Fact Box

Cullinan I Diamond
530.2 carats (106 grams)
Sceptre with the Cross
Tower of London
London

Cullian II Diamond
317.4 carats (63.5 grams)
Imperial State Crown
Tower of London
London

the Cullian I diamond

the Cullian II diamond

Found in South Africa, it was given to King George VII and cut into a number of different diamonds. The two largest diamonds can be found in the Crown Jewels of the United Kingdom.

Working with Diamonds

Many tools used in industry are made with diamonds. This is because they are very strong and can be heated to very high temperatures without breaking. Parts of some space craft are coated with diamond dust to protect them when they are in space.

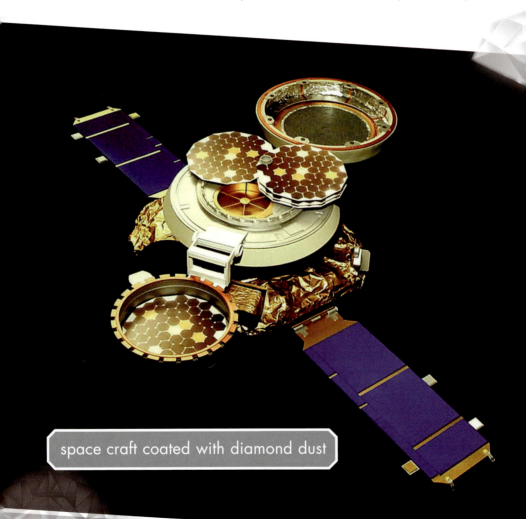

space craft coated with diamond dust

Parts of the space shuttle are protected with diamond dust.

Doctors use scalpels that have a diamond-coated blade because they can make very fine cuts and do not rust.

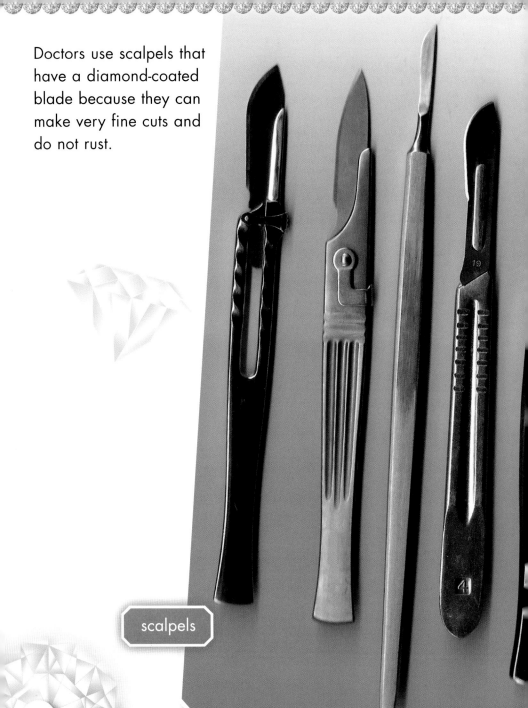

scalpels

diamond drill bit

diamond-coated blade

metal cutter with diamond-coated blade

Tools made with diamonds are also used to make aeroplanes and other engines because they can cut through strong metals.

Growing Diamonds

Scientists can now make diamonds called synthetic diamonds. They are made out of carbon that is pressed together under a lot of pressure and a lot of heat. By growing synthetic diamonds, scientists can keep up with the demand for diamonds in industry.

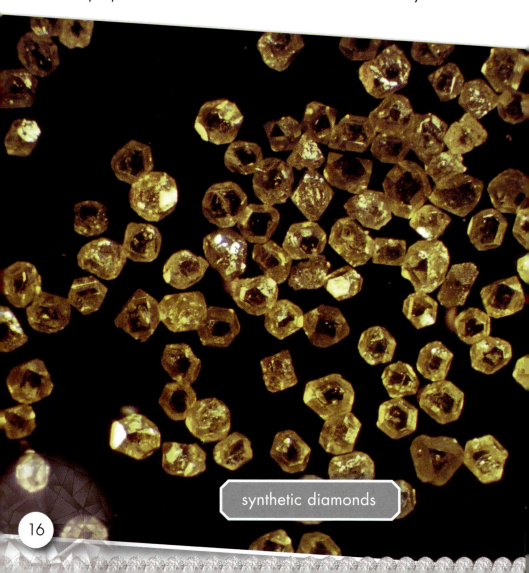

synthetic diamonds

Index

carbon	4, 16
crystal	4
cut	8
diamonds	
alluvial	6
Cullinan	10
Regent	10
synthetic	16
diamond cutter	8
industry	2, 12, 16
pressure	4
river	6
scalpel	14
scientist	16
space	2
space craft	12
swamp	6
stream bed	6
surgery	2
temperature	12
tool	8, 12, 15

Reports

Dramatic Diamonds is a **report**.

A report has a topic:

> **Diamonds**

A report has headings:

> **What Is a Diamond?**

> **Looking for Diamonds**

> **Famous Diamonds**

Some information is put under headings:

FAMOUS DIAMONDS

- The Hope diamond
- The Regent diamond
- The Spoonmaker's diamond

Information can be shown in other ways. This report has . . .

Labels   Bullet Points   Illustrations

Captions   Photographs

Cross-section Diagram

Guide Notes

Title: Dramatic Diamonds
Stage: Fluency

Text Form: Informational Report
Approach: Guided Reading
Processes: Thinking Critically, Exploring Language, Processing Information
Written and Visual Focus: Contents Page, Captions, Labels, Illustrations, Cross-section Diagram, Index

THINKING CRITICALLY
(sample questions)
Before Reading – Establishing Prior Knowledge
- What do you know about diamonds?

Visualising the Text Content
- What might you expect to see in this book?
- What form of writing do you think will be used by the author?

Look at the contents page and index. Encourage the students to think about the information and make predictions about the text content.

After Reading – Interpretation
- Do you think finding a diamond could take a long time? Why do you think that?
- Why do you think diamonds are so popular?
- Do you think that diamonds would be very expensive? Why do you think that?
- Do you think synthetic diamonds would be expensive? Why or why not?
- Do you think alluvial diamonds and synthetic diamonds are very different? Why do you think that?
- What do you know about diamonds that you didn't know before?
- What in the book helped you understand the information?
- What questions do you have after reading the text?

EXPLORING LANGUAGE

Terminology
Photograph credits, index, contents page, imprint information, ISBN number